The Great Spiritual Revolution

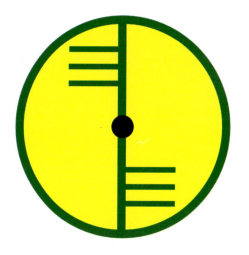

Linda Jane Becker

Copyright © 2009 Linda Jane Becker
All Rights Reserved

No part of this book may be reproduced in any form or by any electronic or mechanical means including information storage and retrieval systems, without permission in writing from the author.

ISBN: 978-1-4276-2892-1

Dear Richard,
You have the power
to create the life
you desire. Use the
[power] it is very powerful.
Dick! Love [...]
Barb

You never change things by fighting the existing reality.
To change something, build a new model that
makes the existing model obsolete.

Buckminster Fuller

iv   Living with Soul ⊕ Linda Jane Becker

Dedicated to Alan

Seeing the Light

It's about 2 a.m. and I am sitting in a room with only the faint light of a television to outline its contents. The television is facing a wall, streaming soft music from its tiny speaker. I am having a serious conversation with my friend Alan's Soul. This conversation goes beyond a heart-to-heart talk. This is a talk about survival and finding the light that nurtures all life. I know if I can get Alan to see this light, it will save his life, even if it doesn't save his body.

I watch his life force ebb and flow like an ocean wave. Weak one moment and strong the next, his body is restless from the pain. He sobs as his fears overwhelm him. I wrap my robe tightly around me and walk towards him, as my heart opens with such compassion I can barely breathe. I slide next to his body, thin and frail, wrapping my motherly arms around him, I hold him close. How can this beautiful Soul not see the light? How could it be, that this man so vibrant a year ago, has not found his way? Why is it that when I point him towards the door with my words, he can't see it?

I have spent a lifetime walking in and out of this light as if it were a strobe light. I am confused at times whether it is the sunlight warming my face or the light of life. Or, are they one in the same? I am bathed in such an expanded knowing of life that other people don't seem to see. Why can't they see the thin strings of life that connect us all together like a spider web? Why can't they feel the pulse of creation? Can't they hear the Universe breathe like I can? Have they not found The Silence yet?

I have never found a common understanding of people and why they behave the way they do. I find the greatest understanding in nature and with creatures of the earth. The Illusion is so consuming if you don't find The Silence within yourself. Find the doorway that holds your light and have the courage to walk through it.

Earlier today, I sat by Alan's side holding his hand while we both watched chemicals drip from a long tube into his arm. A feeling of sickness slowly distorted his posture and the expression on his face. Nausea overcame his ability to breathe deeply; I squeezed his hand as tears streamed down his face.

It's just been another day at an alternative medical clinic in Atlanta Georgia. A clinic that promises a cure for the cancer that is ravishing his body. Day in and day out, he tries everything they recommend, holding on to his dream of a long life.

Tonight the air feels different; the room has a slight scent of rose. The smell of roses always indicates to me, we have company. Not people, but "beings," that live in the light. They communicate to me with so much love. My body vibrates, and my eyes purge with tears, as if flushing away everything that would obstruct my view of their message.

Alan wants to take another shower. I think he wants the showers to wash away the shadow that is haunting him. As he searches for the light, the shadow becomes his blindfold.

I help him out of bed and lead him towards the bathroom. Helping him undress and carefully assisting him to the shower seat, I notice the bruises he has on his chest and back. He received them from a fall yesterday when he was too modest to allow me to see him naked. He decided to shower on his own while I was making him breakfast. He had slipped and fallen on the cold tiled floor. His modesty vanished as I helped his crumbled body stand up.

Making sure he had everything he needed for his shower, I shut the curtain. I sat on the toilet lid, unfolding a towel for him to use when he was ready. The steam filled the room, covering the mirror, trapping us in despair. I prayed as I sat, asking for guidance from our Souls.

When he was finished, I opened the shower curtain and wrapped a towel around his waist. Respecting his need to not feel so vulnerable being naked with someone other than his wife, I covered him with several towels. His heart was heavy with shame and frustration, my heart was heavy with compassion and empathy. I helped him dry his body and then dressed him in a fresh set of pajamas.

Alan wasn't ready to go back to bed, so I guided him to a comfortable chair and covered him with a blanket. I sat in front of him on another chair, knee to knee, holding his hands with our eyes deeply entangled.

I began talking to him about love and the light. How his wife's love was a mirror of his own light. Her love and devotion was the way for his heart to open wide enough to feel the light.

Dedication

I tried in several ways to help him feel this love from her. My voice became an echo of words and feelings.

Suddenly, I could feel the connection I was looking for. I felt his heart connect with mine and the feeling overwhelmed him. My love poured into his heart and it began to open. As it opened, pieces of the protected shield he had placed there so long ago, started floating in the air around us. They were sharp with jagged edges, discolored like rotten food. They were being dismantled and pushed away from us by the light streaming from his heart.

The room fell into complete silence as it filled with light. Our bodies began to tremble as they became consumed with euphoria. Engulfed with this light like a fog in the night, we stopped time, and experienced the illumination of his heart. Tears of joy streamed down our faces, because we knew the miracle that we were experiencing.

As he stabilized with his new opening, the light in the room began to fade. He looked at me in pure joy and said, "I have to call Laurie right now." It was after 4 a.m., but it didn't matter. He had to tell her how much he loved her and how his heart was finally open.

We were overwhelmed with emotions and knew we wouldn't be able to sleep after this experience. So, we had some hot tea and floated in the afterglow, completely speechless.

Alan, I am keeping my promise to share our story with the world. I am thankful for everything you taught me and continue to teach me. I dedicate this book to you.

Namaste

xii   Living with Soul ⊕ Linda Jane Becker

Acknowledgments

To my husband Jim:

You found me wandering aimlessly through life, pulled me into your arms, held on tight and never let go. You supported me in every possible way as I stumbled towards the light. Your unconditional love never wavered, no matter how rough the storms became. I owe you my life many times over. I could never have made it this far without you. I treasure what we have.

To my son Levon:

The moment our eyes met, you smiled at me and my life changed forever. You taught me how to love. You are my computer wizard who makes sure all systems are up and running. Your patience with teaching me how to use the computer no matter how frantic my phone calls became, is nothing short of amazing. Without your hard work, love and dedication to this project, this book would not be done.

To my daughter Heather:

You came into this world, took me by my heart, and raised me with your wisdom, kindness and love. Your gifts are amazing and your compassion incredible. Your continuous belief in this project inspired me on the days I felt lost. As I witness the teachings flowing through you, you become my mirror.

To my dearest friend Stephanie:

You are the true backbone of this book. How courageous of you to take on this project. You taught me to honor the integrity of the teachings, by staying true to the message from the Souls. Your encouragement and constant reminder that I could do this, helped me work on it another day. How you diligently worked through uncountable re-writes. Your unwavering patience with my lack of knowledge of the written word was humbling. You are a true Goddess who dances to the rhythm of Mother Earth.

To my friend Linda:

You took the book and brought it down to earth so the teachings could be understood by the masses. You took a fresh-cut diamond and buffed it to perfection. Your gentleness and faith in me was astounding. You taught me patience with the process and trusting the message. Your heart sings with joy.

To my friend Mary:

Thank you for arriving at the last minute with your expert eyes. You made the words glide across the page.

To my dearest mentor Dawn:

Your honesty and strength never let me hide behind my perceptions. You always went to the core of any issue and made me look at it with truth. You took a stumbling toddler and taught her to run. Our journey together has been extraordinary. Our desire to evolve keeps us ever seeking. You are a great traveling companion.

To my musical healer Tom:

Your beautiful healing music shrouded this whole project with balance, love and peace. As your music played in the background, my space became receptive to the teachings. Your music will heal the world. I feel blessed to have you in my life. Your music is magic.

To my gifted masseuse Shannon:

Your strong healing hands helped keep me comfortable in my cumbersome body. I am forever grateful to your dedication and focus in keeping me balanced. Our friendship has grown over the years as we both strive to become our best. You made this book possible.

Finally, I must thank Grandmother for the gift of healing and R.L. Starr for showing me the way. I am humbled with gratitude to all the Souls who work with me relentlessly, day and night. I am honored and amazed with all the holographic aspects of myself, who have presented themselves as I seek to serve humanity.

In honor of all my friends, patients and students who shared their complicated lives with me. Together we became more, and we evolved towards our greatness.

Living with Soul ⦾ Linda Jane Becker

Contents

Dedicated to Alan v

Acknowledgments.. xiii

Introduction xxiii

We are Masters of Creation xxvii

CHAPTER I
Creation and Reality.. 1
The Silent Pool 3
Creational Beings 7
Choices...11
The Next Reality is Just an Atom Away 15
Infinite Possibilities..19
You are Evolving...27

CHAPTER II
Discovering Self...35
What is in Your Backpack?..37
Finding Balance 40
G.O.D...44

Our Personal Encyclopedia...51

The Chain of Links...54

The Ego: Friend and Foe 59

Loving Yourself 65

The Subject of Truth..74

CHAPTER III

Relationships...79

Desperate Partnerships...83

The Wounded Parent...90

Who are you?...95

Relationships of the Future.......................................100

Bringing Balance to the Sexes 103

Sex in the Future 106

The Challenges We Face..110

CHAPTER IV

Illness, Death and Coming Full Circle 113

The Ultimate Imbalance..116

Death is a New Beginning...121

You Came in Naked and You Will Leave Naked 124

The Disk of Potentiality..140

CHAPTER V

Meditations *143*

Let's Meditate 147
Breathing Deep 151
Erasing the Lines of The Illusion 152
Letting Go 155
Rainbow River Chakra Clearing 157
The Raft Meditation 161

Last Words From The Author 163

About The Author 165

Credentials 167

Contact Information 169

xxii   Living with Soul ◉ Linda Jane Becker

Introduction

We stand poised at the brink of a great Spiritual Revolution--a revolution of personal growth through choice. This revolution must not be ignored if humanity is to evolve into its greatest potential. All of the choices we've made up to this moment have created our lives, if we are not happy--we need to choose differently-- and to live differently.

As a spiritual counselor, I noticed many people facing pivotal choices in their lives. They were standing at a crossroad being forced to make a choice. I also found myself at a crossroad. The more sessions I conducted, the more illuminated my own path became, leading me straight into the Revolution.

In this book and the several that follow, I will guide you through your own personal evolution. I will introduce "The Disk of Potentiality," along with instructions that will empower you to change your life, which will inevitability change the world.

Some of your evolution will be easy, and some will be a challenge. It will be different for everyone, but with a thread of similarity. Be patient. Our classroom is not filled with twenty people, it is filled with billions. We are "all" conscious creators on an evolutionary journey.

Though I live a simple life in this world, I am as big as the sun in the Soul's world. In the silence of my daily meditations, Souls whisper their mysteries to me, secrets they are so willing to share. There have been hundreds of Soul's I've been fortunate to speak with, who have entrusted me with their great wisdom.

As I write this in the early morning on a winter day, I must confess how afraid I am of this mission. Until now, I have kept my gifts gently cupped in my hands, like a butterfly protected from a storm. I ask you to be kind and gentle as I spread my wings and fly into a world of writing and teaching. When we meet, your

Soul will recognize mine, and you will feel me in your heart. All distractions around us will fade away, and our Souls will have a conversation.

Surrounded by Peace
Linda Jane Becker
Winter 2009

xxvi   Living with Soul ⊕ Linda Jane Becker

We are Masters of Creation

This first book presents the idea of an expanded way of thinking and will create new doorways in your mind. My intent is to offer you other choices on how to view your reality. Whatever makes you stretch towards the expansion of your personal evolution, please use it.

I speak a language of the future. This language is about choice, focus, creation, and evolution.

Humanity is ready for the next great surge of its awareness. There is an anxious feeling we are collectively experiencing. The creative force of the Universe is stirring our Souls with excitement. It is time for us to take our focus away from The Illusion by turning it inward and changing our personal reality. I understand how afraid we are of this change. Our fear is based in full ownership. If we are truly creating our reality, then we must own it all, and we must be accountable for all creations manifested in our life.

Are we willing to become fully responsible for our reality *and* this Illusion? Yes, we are ready to take full responsibility for our creations. We are ready to create a new world, starting with our own lives, one by one. I am here to remind you of who you are, and to inspire your conscious evolution. This is my reality and I welcome you to it.

We are masters of creation, we are creators with amnesia.

xxx   Living with Soul ⊕ Linda Jane Becker

Chapter I

Creation and Reality

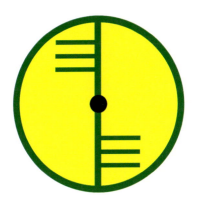

Living with Soul ⊕ Linda Jane Becker

The Silent Pool

Each of us has had a variety of childhood experiences that have shaped who we are today. For many of us, our family experiences were often confusing and sometimes frightening. Over time, our childhood curiosity and innocence were extinguished and replaced by social corruption. We learned many ways to survive, as we walked the labyrinth of childhood. My childhood may have been similar to yours, but I believe my solution for survival was unique. I was five years old, when I became a close friend of the water.

I grew up in a family characterized by abuse, neglect and emotional deprivation. My extreme isolation forced me to find a place within myself that was not filled with intense loneliness. My life was dangerous with chaos. I found safety in the silence of water.

I'd lock the bathroom door, fill the tub as full as I could get it, and then climb in with my clothes still on. I'd sink beneath the water to find The Silence. It is there that my world changed and I felt free from the unpredictable insanity. I'd lie very still and watch the water vibrate from my beating heart. My chest would rise above the water and then sink again. After awhile, I could not feel my body at all. I became the water, which was contained only by the sides of the tub. I realize now that this was my first experience of an expansion in my awareness.

Late at night, safely locked in my room lying under the blankets, I learned to find The Silence. Closing my eyes, I'd lie still, quietly breathing, listening to my heartbeat, and focusing on the vibration it created in my body. In the center of a dark abyss, I saw an outline of a pool. Everything else was black, except for the lights floating in the pool. I'd sit on the edge, watching the lights shimmer. Eventually, I would lean forward and fall into the darkness. Down, down I fell into The Silence until I began to float.

I was free again.

Once, while I was floating in the pool, I was approached by one of the lights. It felt warm and loving as it engulfed me with many colors.

When I returned, I felt different. I had a deeper sense of understanding. I was detached from the world I knew, as a gentle peace stole over me.

I distinctly remember after that experience, standing in the kitchen and watching my father cook breakfast. I knew in that very moment, that everything was a dream; a dream my father was lost in. To this day, very few people recognize we are living in a dream--a dream we are creating.

Most of my life I have tried to keep my balance between The Dream and The Silent Pool. We are shimmering lights from infinity.

*We are from The Silent Pool,
disillusioned by a dream.*

Creational Beings

Source is the absolute origin of everything. Source created the first thought, which established something other than itself, giving birth to duality. Duality allows Source to experience time and space, creating a beginning and an end inside continuous creation. This allows an opportunity for movements of contraction and expansion in the Universe. It is the inhale and the exhale of the breath of life itself.

We are creative expressions of Source. We were creators before this experience, we are creators in this experience, and we will create our experience when this physical body no longer serves us. This is who we are and what we do. We create our reality with every thought and all of our actions.

When I talk about creating with our thoughts, it is not only the words, but the vibrations our thoughts represent. Everything vibrates at a particular frequency. Our personal reality is nothing more than an expression of the individual vibrations we create through our thoughts.

Evolution of the Universe is created by the continuous vibrations we emit. The physical aspect of our world supports our concept of time and space. The earth, being very dense, carries a low and heavy vibration. In a dense reality it takes time for thoughts to manifest.

Whatever we focus on expands in our personal reality. There are more than six and a half billion people creating this experience with all of their thoughts and actions. The diversity of our choices are infinite, therefore this creation has infinite possibilities. Collectively, as creative extensions of Source, we are powerful enough to create a Universe.

Everything is in perfection, because evolution is in perpetual progress. Everything is in total perfection at all times in the Universe. You can only experience chaos in The Illusion.

On this planet, we are expressions of total perfection, because we are constantly creating and evolving.

We are perfect examples of creators creating, evolution in motion.

Choices

The first step in creation is learning to be responsible for your reactions to everything that is happening in your life. The belief that you are a victim is your refusal to take responsibility for your own thoughts. Anybody can be victimized, but it is a person's choice to remain a victim after the experience is over. It is very important to be aware of what you are thinking. Billions of people are creating their own reality from an unconscious state, which creates great chaos in The Illusion.

Life offers us an infinite amount of diversity, which provides endless opportunities for creation and evolution. We were never meant to be the same. How much growth would we achieve if we were all the same? We are meant to be unique. Imagine all the different experiences each human being is having at the same moment? It is incomprehensible. Who could create such a magnificent adventure? We could--and we did.

Where do you think you were before you got here? Where do you think you are going when you leave here? When you hear that internal voice in your head, who is the speaker and who is listening? When you dream at night, who is the observer of the dream and who is really having the experience? All of it is you. We are holographic beings.

If you look at history, you can see how much we have evolved as a species. If you look at humanity as a whole, you can see how we have expanded our consciousness to include much more than mere survival. As our communication with the rest of the world continues to expand, our Oneness with humanity will become clearer. We can create whatever we want, and whatever we don't want. We are limited only by our self-imposed limitations.

Our most powerful obstacles are our resistance to change, and our lack of connection with the wisdom in our Soul. Choice is the most fantastic ability we have. Choose to create the life you want!

Suppose you do not like the neighborhood you live in, or you don't like your job. Why is it so hard to make changes? If you don't like where you live, make a new choice, make a change and move. If you don't like your job, make a new choice, make a change and get a different one. You may be thinking of many reasons why you can't do that, but those reasons are just excuses to stay stuck where you are. If you are afraid of change, you have forgotten your connection to Source, and as a result, you lack confidence in your ability to create. Change is the most fantastic creation we have.

We live in a perfect world, making imperfect choices.

The Next Reality is Just an Atom Away

Reality is defined by our individual focus. Each individual is experiencing a different reality, which is defined by his or her individual focus. All individual realities are occurring simultaneously, here and now. This creates our collective experience. At this moment, there are an infinite amount of realities taking place at the same time, and in the same space.

Take a walk outside with me and I will show you what I mean. Let's start in my backyard, by looking down the valley to the creek. What we see, and what we hear, is determined by where we choose to focus our attention. If we focus on the creek, we can hear the faint sound of the water moving. Focusing above the creek into the trees, we see a beautiful hawk grooming his feathers. Above the trees, circling the sky, there is a blue heron looking for a place to land.

Bring your focus to the butterfly bush next to where we are standing. There are several butterflies sipping nectar, and many bees are buzzing around the blossoms. If we dig up some of the dirt at the base of the butterfly bush, we notice that there are several different kinds of bugs moving around within the soil. Within the soil, there are also many microscopic organisms, which we cannot see with our naked eye. All of these things are going on at the same time, but we are only aware of each of them when we focus on each individually.

The discoveries of quantum physics in the last century have brought into focus entire realities that had previously been unrecognized. Scientists are now developing theories which prove the existence of multiple parallel Universes, energy fields, and black holes. If these theories can be proven true, then everything we think we know about existence and the nature of the universe is changed by this new focus.

Anything one person does, affects everything. There is only the "appearance" of separation, because we believe ourselves to be separate beings. On an energetic level, there are no boundaries. You may not be able to recognize the change on a conscience level. Still, the change has affected all of existence. Infinity travels both ways. It travels toward the infinitely small, and toward the infinitely large.

Even destruction is a form of creation, because creation actually has no opposite. There are atoms projecting a manifestation, and there are atoms that have not yet manifested. Atoms contain intelligence. Even when they haven't gathered together to create a manifestation, they are still creating themselves.

I define Universe as, "you in reverse."

Infinite Possibilities

It is possible to change our reality by making different choices. We can make choices from an infinite range of realities, but we must first learn how to do it. Our thoughts and beliefs about what is real, creates our reality. We must believe we already are what we are trying to create.

Our reality shifts when we shift our focus, thoughts and actions. Even though you are programmed to accept who you are, you are also in constant change. Your beliefs can change as you change your focus, thoughts and actions.

You must remember that you are constantly changing your reality, as you shift your focus. By shifting your focus, everything around you will begin to shift and change in your reality. If you want to be a more loving person, all you have to do is to be more loving in your thoughts and your actions. The people in your life, who are willing to join you in your new reality, will change to fit your idea. The people who resist your change will capture your focus, pulling you back into your old behavior. Your desire to stay connected to a person or situation oftentimes impedes your desire for change. You have to be willing to let go of everything that blocks your focus and stagnates your evolution. Once you are willing to let go, the people who resist your new choices will simply pull away from your new reality.

We are very powerful beings. As we focus on any one thing, we will bring it into manifestation. That is why we have been told over the years to surround ourselves with people who inspire us, and people we consider to be our heroes. Focusing on people who inspire us, will in itself, keep us evolving toward greatness.

Movies, books and even music, tell us about other people's realities and experiences, and how they cope with them. For years, I have used the multi-theater concept as a teaching tool.

Imagine you are at a movie theater which has an unlimited choice of movies to choose from. In one theater, there is a drama. In another, there is an adventure, or a mystery, or maybe a western. Just down the hall, there is a theater with a romantic comedy, and another filled with horror or war.

Just as in life, this is your buffet of realities from which you can choose. Therefore, you choose to go inside the movie theater that offers the experience you want to undergo. When the movie has your full attention, you become a part of the experience. After awhile, if you decide you don't want to be a part of this movie anymore, you can choose to leave this experience for a different one.

Look over your other choices, there are an infinite number of choices you can make. If you don't like your reality, make a new choice. Choose a different reality. It is that simple. You choose what you want to experience by choosing which movie, which reality, you want to assume. If it isn't what you want, simply make a different choice. We slip in and out of a multitude of realities every day.

Chapter I - Creation and Reality 21

To illustrate my point, let's say that you hate driving in rush hour traffic to get to work every day. There are many things that can happen to change this. You could lose your job. Your car might not start one morning. Your alarm could malfunction, and you could wake up *after* rush hour traffic. You could get sick, or wreck your car and be unable to work.

Good things could happen too. Someone could offer to car pool and do all the driving if you would share the gas expense. Your boss could adjust your work hours so that you would be able to drive to work at a different time. You could get a promotion that allows you to work from home. Do you see the possibilities of change?

We are holographic beings. This means that we are simultaneously experiencing an infinite number of realities. We anchor ourselves in this reality by our focus. You are experiencing every choice you could possibly make on every level, in alternate realities. On top of that, it is all happening in this exact moment.

Imagine a music CD. On this CD there is a symphony. This symphony has one million notes in it. I like to call this "The Symphony of Your Soul." In creating music, there must be notes, and there also must be spaces between the notes. Most people think the musical notes create the music, but it is the space between the notes that actually creates the melody and rhythm of the music. If there were no spaces between the notes, then there would be only one continuous tone, and not the sound of music. In order to experience music, there must be a focus on the notes and a focus on the spaces between the notes.

Your individual point of focus is what connects you to the particular note you experience. Since this symphony is "The Symphony of Your Soul," then every note in your symphony is an alternate reality, where you have made different choices that have created many different experiences. The spaces between the alternate realities are what keep them separate from one another. Where you place your focus

Chapter I - Creation and Reality   23

is the experience you are witnessing in any given moment. This is the life you are experiencing here and now.

Our ability to move our focus is what gives us the power to experience an infinite number of realities. We are creating all of the realities by making different choices. This is a very personal experience. You don't need to get into a rocket ship and travel through a worm hole in order to experience a different reality. You can move easily from one reality to another, just by changing your focus.

You have an infinite amount of choices and an infinite amount of realities. Anything you could possibly want to experience, you are experiencing in at least one of your realities. You don't have to create what you want. You just have to focus on what you want. All of your choices have already been created; you are connected to all of your alternate realities. Every choice you make in this reality affects all of the other realties, and vice versa.

Think of the last time you misplaced your car keys. When you were ready to leave, you looked around for your keys and discovered they were not where you had left them. You looked in several places you thought they could be, but still you couldn't find them. You retraced your footsteps and then finally went back to check a place where you had already looked several times before. Suddenly, you find your keys. Now, do you think it was you or your keys that switched realities?

Every step you place on this earth, changes it forever.

You are Evolving

Your Soul has come here to create evolution. Your Soul creates evolution by giving you the power to manifest in this world. The experience of challenge, choice and surprise is what life on this planet is all about. This is why enlightenment, being One with Source, is really not our goal while we are here. Before you arrived here you were One with Source. To contribute to evolution, you agreed to fall into "The Illusion of Separation" with Source, in order to create with thoughts.

While in this experience of separateness, you seek Oneness, because you yearn to rejoin Source. Your Soul is Source experiencing The Illusion of Separation. It only appears that you are separate while you are in a physical body. We are never truly separate from Source, because we are the living creative expressions of Source.

You came here, to this life experience, fully equipped. Every question you have can be answered by your Soul. Do you think you would take a trip like this and not come prepared? Where do you think you packed everything? Many of us are so distracted by The Illusion that we think everything we need is outside of us. All of our answers are within us.

When you fell into this illusion, you became a part of it without remembering your connection to Source. The Soul is a spark of Source, being expressed through humanity. You are this beautiful spark encased in a physical body, so you can have a physical experience in a physical world. This beautiful spark is in everyone and in everything.

Only when you see the light within yourself can you see it in another. When I see a homeless person, I see the same light in that person as I see in myself. The only difference between the two of us is in the choices we have made. Every choice we make creates our life experience. The magic of The Illusion is that by making different choices, we have the ability to create a different life, *every day*.

You are responsible for keeping your body safe. That is why the Ego was created. We needed a part of us to protect the physical body, so we created the Ego. The Ego is our *bodyguard.* It is an aspect of us that is in charge of keeping the body safe and alive. The Ego created the personality so it could interact in the environment, and interact with other personalities. The Ego lives only in The Illusion. Your Soul lives outside of The Illusion, witnessing the experience of The Illusion.

Your Soul is not restricted by The Illusion. Your Soul needed something that could fully embrace The Illusion so that it could be affected by the full experience of The Illusion. In this way your Soul has a complete physical experience.

The Ego's only job is to keep our body safe and alive. Basically, it simply gathers and stores information about its environment. The Ego categorizes, judges, speculates, calculates and reacts to the environment through the personality.

Chapter I - Creation and Reality

Personalities are used to interact within The Illusion, stimulating situations to gain more information for the Ego. Unconsciously, we know that everything is in constant change and movement, so we continuously check to see what has changed. The Ego is very afraid of change, because any change creates vulnerability and insecurity. Our focus is directed outside of us all the time, because the Ego is always gathering information to guide the actions of the personality. Everything that exists outside of us is an illusion, created by the collective consciousness.

Whenever I am drawn too heavily into The Illusion, and lose sight of who I really am, I sit down and close my eyes. After a couple of deep breaths, I start erasing all the lines that create the appearance of separation. I begin with erasing the edges that define my body, and then I erase the lines around the room I am in. I then move on to erase the lines around the building, the city, the state, the country, the planet, and all the way out into the universe, until all of the lines are gone. Then I sit in the beautiful vibration of Source, the Oneness that is there when all the lines of separation are gone. Through this expansion, I stay connected to Source.

Whenever I want to return to The Illusion, I start redrawing the lines. When the lines are all replaced, I feel completely different. Whatever thoughts had previously seemed so important have now lost their value, and my thinking is extremely clear. I call this "moving into the eye of the storm."

The storm can rage all around me, and some of the time it will pull me in. When I realize I am experiencing the storm, which means I realize that I am experiencing The Illusion of Separation, I make the choice to get my eraser out. This is how I stay in contact with what is real for me.

Our Souls live outside The Illusion. Our mind lives in both places. Our mind is our connection to both The Illusion and to Source. Our mind has the ability to work both inside and outside of The Illusion. Since the mind can

Chapter I - Creation and Reality 31

work in both places, it can draw energy from Source and manipulate it into manifestation. It does this all the time.

This is how we create our personal reality. Imagine everything is like a mirage, or like a diamond with an infinite amount of facets, each facet you look into shows you something different.

Our eyes are like windows into The Illusion.
They see what we want them to see.

Chapter I - Creation and Reality

Living with Soul ✪ Linda Jane Becker

CHAPTER II

Discovering Self

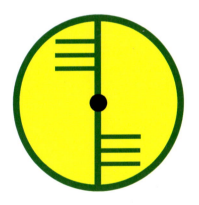

Living with Soul ❀ Linda Jane Becker

What is in Your Backpack?

Throughout my years of working with students, I have discovered that the majority of them could not move forward in their own evolution, because they could not leave their past behind. In a deep meditation one morning, I saw myself sitting under a beautiful tree near the top of a mountain. A young woman walked towards me carrying a very heavy backpack. I asked her to sit down and rest awhile.

"Where are you going," I asked?

She said, "I am going to the top of the mountain."

"What is in your backpack?"

She looked at me very surprised and said, "What backpack?"

I stood up and helped her remove her heavy pack, lowering it to the ground between us. She unzipped the bag and began taking out rocks of varied shapes and sizes. One at a time she piled them in a stack in front of me. Although she had no idea where they came from, she was very relieved to leave the burden behind and continue on her journey with an empty pack.

Time passed, and she approached me again with a full backpack. We sat down together and once again emptied the heavy pack. We noticed that both piles of rocks looked exactly alike. We agreed she should leave the backpack behind, and try again.

Many hours went by when she appeared for the third time. This time I noticed her pants pockets were heavy with rocks. She was shocked to see me, and she noticed that her backpack was still sitting where she had left it. I pointed to her pockets, and she began to empty them, placing the rocks on the ground.

We decided if she was going to make it to the top, she needed to tear the pockets out of her pants. That way if she picked up any more rocks, they would fall through the holes in her pants, and land back on the ground.

I waited for awhile, and she did not return. I began to journey up the mountain myself. As I traveled, I saw many rocks on the path. However, the farther I walked the fewer rocks I saw. When I reached the top, I saw her sitting in the sunshine, completely naked. I asked, "Where are your clothes?"

"Everything I carried was a burden," she said.

In that moment, I realized if we want to reach the top of the mountain, we must be brave enough to strip ourselves of all our burdens. So I ask you, what is in your backpack, and are you brave enough to be completely naked in this world?

Chapter II - Discovering Self   39

Finding Balance

When our Egos are triggered by an experience, the vibration that we emit connects to that same frequency within the collective consciousness. This, in turn, energizes our emotions around the experience. Instead of staying neutral in the experience so we can make a balanced choice to respond, our Egos immediately react, creating chaos and confusion. In this way, our Egos participate in energizing the situation, instead of discovering a solution.

In order to respond with choice in a situation, we need to be fully present in the moment. Many people have told me they had no choice in a given situation. This is simply not true. You may have "limited" choices in a situation, but you will "always" have a choice. Sometimes your choice may be as simple as viewing the situation differently. Your Ego may tell you that you have no other choice, but remember your Ego lives in The Illusion, and is unaware of your connection to Source.

When we react in a situation without considering our choices, distortion and chaos will always arise. Our life is a continuous string of choices, one choice leading into the next. Since we have been making choices all of our lives, many of the choices we make can occur in a split second.

We usually aren't aware of our choices as we are making them. When choices are an automatic reaction from our Ego, we are no longer in the present moment. We are being guided by our past, and this is a form of sleep walking. We are unconscious and lost in The Illusion.

We are here to be infinite creators of the Universe. What a boring existence we have come to accept when we forget our ability to create. We have been living inside The Illusion for so long that we have stopped looking for anything beyond it. How constricted we have become from our various fears.

We are so lucky to be here having this experience, living a life in this fantastic physical body. We are in a world of our own creation as creative masters. Humans have lost sight of how magnificent they are.

Now is the time to awaken and remember.

Chapter II - Discovering Self

G.O.D.

God is not something, or someone that exists outside of yourself, or is separate from you. God resides in you. Stop looking outside of yourself for someone to praise, or someone to blame for your experience. Go inside yourself for all you seek, and realize the creator that you are. My definition of G.O.D. is *"Go Only Deep."* Nothing is outside of you except The Illusion, and The Illusion is only a representation of history, thoughts manifesting his-story or her-story.

Do you think we would take a trip to earth unprepared? We came fully equipped. Do you think there was anything you forgot to pack? We are completely whole. Since we came in naked where do you think we packed everything? Everything we will ever need for this journey is already within us.

Please stop looking outside of yourself for someone who has the power that you seek. You do not need to give your power to God, Angels, Spirits, or Buddha. They are not separate from you. Collectively, they "are" you. They are within you. To connect with them, you must *Go Only Deep.*

Remember, energy can never be destroyed. Energy can only change in form. If energy is never destroyed, then all energy from all thoughts and personalities are still here. They do not evaporate.

Your body will be absorbed by the earth when you are finished with it. Everything that was created here will stay here. Your Soul will move on and continue creating. Your personality will stay a part of the collective consciousness, living in a non-physical world of its own creation, readily available to assist the people it left behind.

Take a moment and think about the majority of thoughts that concern you. You think about the weather, your spouse, sex, your family and friends. You think about your job, your car, your neighbors, and what's in the news. You concern yourself with politics, religion, your body, someone else's body, your diet, your health, your clothes, shopping, and so forth. It is all just a lot of thinking about things outside of you, creating and feeding The Illusion.

How often do you take a break from The Illusion to experience The Silence, and to have an experience in this moment? Stopping your journey for a moment, and resting? This experience existed before you got here, and it will continue to exist after you're gone. You existed before you got here, and you will continue to exist after you leave, because your energy lives forever.

You may think, "Oh, when I am not here, I am there." Where is there? This thinking creates the experience of duality, the notion that you're limited to either here or there. When here is the only place that exists, then there is nowhere to go. Even when your body dies, whether you are buried in the ground or cremated, you are still here. Whether you are rotting flesh, or dust in the wind. It is only a change of form. You don't go *anywhere*. You just have another experience.

When The Illusion of Separation is gone, because your body has died, you will once again experience the totality of Oneness with Source. No separation will exist--only wholeness. It is true for you now, as well. There *is* no separation, only The Illusion of Separation.

If we could lose our fear around death, we would live our lives more fully. From the moment we take on a physical body, death of that physical organic form is inevitable. Life is what you create between birth and death. You create your life with every thought and with every action. You can create *paradise*, or you can create *hell*. You can create joy, or you can create sadness. Your choices are infinite, they always have been, and they always will be.

You give your power away to the unconscious side of creation when you believe life is just "happening" to you. When you do not use your energy for the purpose of consciously creating your life, that energy becomes unconscious and contributes to the chaos in The Illusion. Unconscious energy is used by anyone who is seeking more energy.

When you throw away your energy, it just floats around waiting to be used by anyone. If you want to just let life happen to you, this energetically puts you into the frequency of a victim. This is like driving a car without a steering wheel.

If you are not using your abundance of energy responsibly, you are freely giving it away for *anyone* to use. Energy continuously flows through us. We can make use of it for intentional purposes or not. It is up to us to choose what we want to do with the gift. If we choose not to use this energy responsibly and with conscious intention, we are choosing to just let life happen to us. The unused energy will continue moving, until it is used by someone or something else.

When you see chaos in the world, ask yourself how much of the potential creative energy you decided *not* to use, might be contributing to the creation of this chaos. This is where being personally responsible for your life is so important. If you are willing to own all of your thoughts, words and actions, then you will not be a victim of unconscious thinking.

When you take responsibility for your experience as a creator, you will not be a victim, and life will not just happen to you. Become a conscious creator and create your life with "intent." When you use your share of energy to create your reality, then you enhance The Illusion by your thoughts and actions. In order to create a life you want, all you need to do is figure out what you really want, and focus on it. I know it is hard to believe that you can be so powerful to manifest your reality, but it is true.

Understand that *anything* and *everything* you could ever want, is already here. Our thoughts come from a collective field of thought. There are no original thoughts. Whatever you are thinking, someone else is thinking it too. You are not alone, even in your thoughts.

Chapter II - Discovering Self 49

Life is an action state of awareness.

Our Personal Encyclopedia

The definition of the word encyclopedia is "various topics dealing with a range of human knowledge." Encyclopedia is the perfect word to describe the information the Ego uses to function in The Illusion through the personality. Everything you know is stored and used as a reference by the Ego. Everyone has a personal encyclopedia. Everyone's encyclopedia is unique. This is what makes each of us different, and is a catalyst for evolution.

We are continually updating our personal encyclopedia. We reinforce a belief or we adjust it with every thought. Our encyclopedia is constantly being upgraded and changed by what we observe and experience in The Illusion.

Our personal encyclopedia is created by our life experiences, and what we have learned from other people. Many people have similar experiences, causing their encyclopedia to have comparable beliefs. When we interact with people, we influence their encyclopedia. Unfortunately, many of us believe we *are* our personal encyclopedia. Our greatest power is in having complete control over our encyclopedia. When you use your power to extract an old belief and replace it with a new one, it is possible to actually change the way you think or believe about something.

Most people believe this is difficult to do, but it is not. It is a simple process to change anything about yourself, which you choose to change. You are the most powerful creator in the Universe. In fact, you *created* this Universe--and you continue to create it with every thought.

All thoughts create, and they are not exclusive to our experience here on earth. In the big picture, even earth is an illusion, because it appears to be separate from everything else. If you want to see the big picture, you must get out your eraser and start erasing the lines of separation.

Who are you, really?

Chapter II - Discovering Self

The Chain of Links

Sometimes, a particularly obsessive thought or belief keeps recurring in someone's reality. When this occurs, the object of their obsession may seem to pop up constantly in their life. This occurs because when we keep our focus on that one thought or belief, we allow it to continually manifest in our reality. Our thoughts can loop through our mind, playing automatically without conscious intention. Like the greeting on your answering machine, the same loop will continue to play until we consciously change the message.

This is a form of spiritual sleep walking, and it is the fundamental reason why we continue to *react* instead of to *respond*. When we react in a given situation, we are not making a conscious choice. We are only making a programmed reaction to certain stimuli or vibrations. We group similar vibrations together wherever possible, in order to apply a consistent reaction to a situation. I call this a "chain link reaction."

Many times, I've worked with students on a specific emotional reaction. When we worked through the reaction and changed the vibration by responding with awareness, we healed many other reactions, as well as the one we were focusing on. This is why I believe there is a running connection, in terms of energy, like a chain of links.

I met a woman many years ago who had been diagnosed with Trichophobia (fear of hair). When she was a young girl, she was camping in the woods with her parents when a bear attacked the family camped next to them, killing their young son. As her parents comforted the family until help arrived, the young girl became very silent and distant. For many years she sought help from therapists, but her condition worsened. By the time we met she was depressed, suicidal, and on several medications. The bear attack was the first link in the chain, but not necessarily the strongest.

We categorize our memories into groups with similar feelings. The more memories we have attached to an emotion, the longer the chain, and the harder it is for us to pinpoint the strongest link. This is why, when we have an emotional experience and try to discuss it, we often get lost in the pain, allowing many other painful experiences to surface. The links in the chain allow us to connect to other links, confusing us as to the exact topic, as we remain in the emotional feeling. The confusion overwhelms us, and we lose our ability to focus on where the *real* pain originated.

It takes a bit of digging to get to the strongest link in the chain. You will discover that it is rarely just one thing. The most powerful memory is not always the strongest link in the chain. There are several links supporting each other, and that's why it looks like a chain to me.

In the story of the woman and the bear attack, it took months to uncover each link in the chain. Together, we uncovered one clue at a time, until we found the strongest link. Even though she was traumatized by the bear attack, we discovered that the strongest link occurred when she was bitten by her classroom mascot—a furry, little guinea pig! When we discovered this, all the links in the chain began to dissolve, one at a time, until her fears were gone.

I have discovered that these links begin to form soon after birth. Fear is usually the first emotion we have, which creates the first link. All through our life, we fear the unknown, adding more links to the chain. That is why change is so difficult for us. If we had the mindset that life is an adventure which guarantees constant change, and always contains the element of surprise, we would embrace change and not fear it.

Do you remember what it is like to see the world through a child's eyes, not yet so filled with The Illusion?

The Ego: Friend and Foe

The Ego protects our body, and is our best friend if we are in a dangerous situation. It is a necessary component for us in a physical body. The Ego is our bodyguard, without it we could not survive. The Ego's energy flow is fear, which is the energy used for survival. This enables us to keep our body alive in The Illusion.

Many of us like to use the Ego as our excuse for "reacting" to life instead of being in the moment, and "responding." The Ego reacts quickly and draws conclusions instantly. When we judge other people, we are using our Ego. This is very interesting to think about because when we use the Ego in our judgment of other people, it is actually *our* Ego judging *their* Ego.

When an individual's focus is dominated by his Ego, then his personal focus is on full alert for survival. This is extremely dangerous for everyone. When the Ego is totally in control, everyone else becomes the enemy, and eradication will begin. At those times, the gap between what the Ego perceives as "me," and what the Ego perceives as "them," becomes so large that nothing matters but the Ego's perception of "me." This is complete lack of any recognition of our Oneness.

Here is an example of the Ego at work. Imagine that you quickly step into a crowded elevator. You turn and face the door, as the elevator begins to move. While you are standing there, someone or something jabs you in the back. Naturally, you move away from the intrusion.

Then your personality has an emotional reaction. You turn and look at what has disturbed you. The first thing you see is a man standing there with an armful of books. As you turn, he apologizes for bumping you. You nod your head, and start rationalizing the emotions that have just erupted within you.

Now, what if you had turned around and saw that it was a tearful woman holding a box which looked like all of her personal belongings from her desk? You would assume that this woman had just lost her job, and your emotions around a person losing their job would change your emotions about the incident.

Now, imagine that when you turn around, you see a small boy, about the age of five. He has no hair on his head. The IV pole he is holding is what actually poked you in the back. He looks up at you, and asks if you want to see the drawing he made of his family. What emotions are you feeling? Now think of these three different scenarios from a different point of view.

Instead of a "neutral" point of view, as in the previous example, imagine viewing the situation from an "emotional" point of anger. What if, right before you got into the elevator, you had an argument with a nurse about the care of a loved one? You enter the elevator after your heated conversation, with the issue unresolved. Rethink these three scenarios with this emotion forefront. How might your reactions be different?

Next, let's imagine you've just spent the last hour meditating in the hospital's chapel, before you entered the elevator. How might your reaction be affected by this experience? What if you had spent the last hour in the nursery, holding and rocking newborns before you got into the elevator? How does this feel different?

This is an example of how four different emotions, generated from a past experience, control our perception of the present moment. First you experienced the elevator story with neutral emotions, then anger, peace, and love. When you bring your past into the present moment, it alters your ability to respond authentically in the moment.

The same incident happened, but by using your emotions, judgments and encyclopedia, you had different reactions of how you perceived the experience.

Do you see how wonderful your Ego was in the moment you were poked, pulling you away from the pain? Your Ego is the aspect of you that your personal life experience has programmed to protect you and keep you safe. Our Egos react to any given situation in accordance to how balanced an individual is at the time.

The more unbalanced a person is, the more severe that person's reaction will be in the situation. If an individual is in complete balance, then that person will not "react," they will "respond." When we are off balance, we allow our Egos to facilitate our emotions.

Your Ego is here to protect your physical body, and to keep it safe from whatever danger presents itself from The Illusion. Your heart helps you express love and compassion from the Soul. We must find our balance between them.

Everything is connected.

Loving Yourself

It is nobody's responsibility to love you. Loving you is not the responsibility of your mom, dad, husband, wife, daughter, son, aunt, uncle, dog, cat, co-workers, boss, or friend. Let me say it again. It is absolutely no one's responsibility to love you. It is one hundred percent *your* responsibility to love yourself.

Giving away your power for happiness to anyone else will create a disaster. Nobody knows what makes you happy better than you. Why would you entrust someone else with your life's happiness? It is no one's responsibility to make you happy, even someone who loves you.

We are all too willing to hand our personal power over to someone else, making them responsible for us. It is no wonder that so many people are unhappy, and blaming others for their misery. Be responsible for your own happiness. Do not give your power away to *anyone.*

When "need" enters your relationship it will destroy the love you share, and replace it with a distorted obsession, forcing the love you have to grossly disfigure. In our society, we are taught that all of our happiness is received from outside of ourselves, and that it is everyone's job to give us what we think we need to make us happy.

Throughout our lives, we navigate through endless loops of continuous want and need, which are constantly stimulated by The Illusion. When we find that we cannot get our needs met through others, many of us try to sooth this pain by turning to self medication or substance abuse, to which we become addicted. Our endless search for love and happiness only results in a lifetime full of disappointments.

Society sets confusing rules regarding who, how, when, and where we can find love. Many of us believe that to love ourselves is to be considered selfish and conceited. In order to find true happiness, we must learn that all happiness is created by self love. We must learn to step out of our Ego-driven personality, and slide into our hearts for the wisdom that lives within our Soul.

If you want to experience self love, you must see beyond The Illusion. Close your eyes and breathe slowly. Allow any outside stimulus a chance to drift away. Listen to your own rhythm. Learn to recognize the light that is within yourself, so you can recognize the light within everyone else. Without this recognition and connection, your suffering and the suffering of others will continue in The Illusion.

It's easy to lose your sense of self in a world of continuous noise. Distractions are designed to keep us constantly focused outward into The Illusion. When you take the time to pause and listen to your breath, your body moves into a natural stillness. Listen to your own heartbeat. Follow the sound. It will lead you to the most beautiful peace you have ever felt, and within that peace you'll find all the love you could ever want.

Chapter II - Discovering Self

When you came into this experience called life, you brought love with you from Source. You are not the personality that your mind created in order to interact within The Illusion. You are the Soul, and you are wise with the wisdom of the Soul. Your Ego has done such a great job keeping all of your attention focused in The Illusion. You have lost sight of the real you, and you have forgotten your reason for existing in this experience.

Expand your understanding. Come to terms with your creative force, and accept that everything is a part of you. I once read that cosmologists have no clue what seventy percent of the Universe consists of. They agree it contains a substance unlike any other and they agree that something is there. This "something" is Source, conscious of itself manifesting through thought.

Outlines and edges are what give us the appearance that there is a separation between everything. This sense of separation enables us to continue to identify with The Illusion. Each Soul, as it moves through our collective pool of energy, never experiences separation. There is only "the illusion of separation," as defined by the perceptions of our Ego-driven personalities.

Source energy vibrates in the frequency of love. We have the ability to consciously connect to this frequency of energy, but in order to do that, we must first disconnect from the distractions within The Illusion. When we connect to the frequency of our Soul, and love through our hearts, this connection gives us everything we need. It is our true Source of guidance.

When our energy is focused through the heart, it is our nature to support and nurture each other. When our energy is focused through the Ego, then we react from an instinct to survive. In either circumstance, our basic need is always to love and to be loved. It is this energy of love that expands our Universe. Source loves without conditions or attachments.

Over the years, cultural brainwashing has distorted our understanding of love, making it almost unrecognizable. The intense state of fear many of us live in today, has nearly erased our memory of love. Love comes straight from the Soul, through the heart, and into our reality.

Love flows out through you, from Source, and touches countless other Souls. Like water moving through a riverbed, love flows through you and you become the love. Loving from this place allows you to reconnect with the wisdom of your Soul, and to experience Oneness with Source.

When we take the time to silence our outside world, we discover a whole new level of reality. Imagine that you are standing in front of a huge field of wild flowers, on a warm, sunny day. As far as you can see, there are beautiful flowers in full bloom. In this exact moment, if you are totally present, their beauty will consume you. As they dance in the wind, you connect with their pool of love. The field of flowers is not separate from you. In fact, the field of flowers is an expression of love. It is pure beauty, perfection in expression.

If you take the time, you can see the beauty in everything that is around you. *Everything* vibrates with love. It is only our perception that distorts it.

Our reality is molded by what we focus on with our thoughts. If you turn on the television and watch the news, which is totally focused in The Illusion, it will be difficult to see the love around you. I call watching the news "emotional suicide." The vibration of the frequency of television alone is so dense, that it takes me days to raise my vibration so I can even attempt to experience the frequency of love again.

It is the same for newspapers, movies, books, and people. Don't get me wrong, occasionally I watch television, enjoy a movie, or read a good book. However, I do these things with the understanding that it will take me some time to balance myself afterwards.

I also understand that what I *do* watch or read, will influence and alter my perception of The Illusion. So, I choose carefully what I allow into my reality. I would advise you to do the same. Stay conscious of your surroundings, and pay close attention to what you allow yourself to experience.

Steps for creation:
Thought--(thinking the thought)
Emotion--(fueling the thought)
Movement--(doing the thought)

The Subject of Truth

Nothing has been quite so exciting for the Ego, as its search for truth. This is especially true for anything that the Ego believes to be the "One Truth." The Ego defines truth as safety. The more truth or information it knows, the better the Ego believes it can protect the body within The Illusion.

One of the hardest things for your Ego to refrain from is its constant search for truth. When you continually search for truth, you are reinforcing your Ego's belief that you are not whole, that you are not safe. It creates a feeling of insecurity if you continually search for the evidence of truth. If you look within The Illusion, for someone to tell you something that will make you feel safe, then you will never feel safe. Truth does not lie within The Illusion.

The expression, "everything is in divine order," can bring a feeling of comfort and safety to many of us. However, when we believe in this statement, we are actually giving our power away to something supreme, outside of ourselves. If we understand the statement to mean that "divine order" translates to evolution, and all of evolution is in order, then we are powerful in this knowing.

Another favorite expression that many of us have become accustomed to using as a form of acceptance is "everything happens for a reason." If the "reason" is because people make choices that affect other people, then we own our power, and it becomes a knowing. If we believe that everything happens for a reason, and that reason is because there is something supreme in charge of everything, then we are still giving our power away.

There is no "One Truth." Truth is flexible and changes as we evolve. Truth is an evaluation, a judgment. There are examples of this throughout our history. What was true yesterday may not be true today. What we consider truth is always distorted by The Illusion. The truth you seek to help you clarify who you are cannot be found in The Illusion.

Chapter II - Discovering Self   75

This truth is already within you. It is your inner knowing, the wisdom you brought here with you from Source.

Ever since God was placed outside of us, and made supreme, we have felt empty. Ever since we have forgotten that the truth is within, we have been on an endless search for fulfillment. As long as we believe God is *outside* of us we will always feel powerless. God has *never* been separate from us.

Become the creator you are meant to be, by becoming One with God, the God that resides in every cell of your body. Connecting with Source is the only way to find your wisdom.

Remember my definition of God is "Go Only Deep."

Chapter III

Relationships

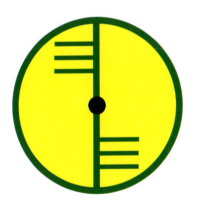

Come Sail with Me

I left the dock before the sun was up.

I am searching for you with all my heart.

The breeze is gentle and the
sails are fully open.

The ripples I leave in the water
behind me carry away with them old
memories of sadness and destitution.

I pray the wind will lead me to you.

I have so little to offer, only this
boat with scars so deep, the
water is slowly seeping in.

How do I know you are there?

I just know.

Is it a dream, or is it a
vision of the future?

This, I do not know.

Am I bleeding because of you, or
because I don't have you?

Will you cherish the love I give, or
will you throw it into the abyss?

I come confused and complicated.

I lost the map so long ago.

The strange sounds in the
darkness frighten me.

I have no life jacket.

I can no longer see the light on the dock.

I have arrived at the point of no return.

This is my last attempt to find you.

I know when I find you, I
will also find me.

The sun is bringing light to the
sky and hope to my heart.

In the distance I see a boat
sailing towards me.

Is it you?

Desperate Partnerships

Through the years, I have worked with many couples, as well as people who are single. Each person was looking for the same thing. They were each seeking the "perfect" relationship, or one that was perfect for them. Not everyone had the same description of a perfect relationship, but they all wanted it to be now, and easy.

Over and over again, I continually saw how much old baggage each person brought into their new relationships.

Desperate people will make the decision to seek a relationship in order to distract their focus from their own growth. Most people have a specific idea of what they want. Some people even have their desires all itemized on paper. And many expect to find the perfect partner, when they have yet to find a balanced relationship with themselves.

When we are in balance, we naturally slip into the process of evolving through self love. When we are filled with love for ourselves, we realize what magnificent beings we truly are. Sharing our life with someone else is still enticing, but it is no longer mandatory.

Our traditional concept of wanting someone to spend our life with, is very narrow and limiting. Why do we think there is only one person for us to find? Why do we believe just one partner could meet all of our needs? There are billions of people on this planet. Why would you want to share your life with just one? Do you think one person could complement all the facets of you?

Deeply ingrained in our consciousness is the belief we must have a life partner. We want someone to witness and participate in our life, giving our life more meaning. To evolve into a more balanced human being, we must first become whole within ourselves. To evolve as humanity, we must first evolve individually.

Relationships are a wonderful place for each of us to evolve into our greatest creation. Relationships can provide the most fertile ground for us to grow and understand who we truly are. It is an excellent place to heal our past, and to create our future.

There is great confusion about how to have a balanced partnership without losing ourselves in the process. Most people want their own way, making it a daily battle of who wins and who loses.

Often in partnerships there is one who takes control, and one who surrenders. The greatest relationships have total balance. I don't mean fifty-fifty, but that both partners need to be willing to give one hundred percent--all of the time. Each partner is responsible for making sure neither one dominates the relationship.

The most common reason for unhappiness in all things, including relationships, is fear. People find it difficult to trust and to be honest with each other. Are you honest with yourself? Do you feel safe within yourself? If not, how is it possible to feel safe within a relationship? We all hide behind our wounded past.

Chapter III - Relationships

Take a moment to write out your own list of attributes that you desire in another, and then apply the list to yourself. How many of those qualities do *you* possess? Many people set unrealistic expectations, guaranteeing they will not find anyone capable of "filling their order." It's like buying a cake mix and expecting the cake to be already baked.

Each of us has to feel safe--without fear-- in our relationships, or we cannot be authentic. We cannot be honest. A balanced partnership creates an energy that represents both partners. This balanced energy is synergetic. It creates an energy that is greater than the sum of either of its parts.

Once you commit to being in a relationship of any type, you must agree on the guidelines. When guidelines are established in the beginning, it provides you with a solid foundation on which to build.

All of us were raised in families who had their own set of rules. When you move into a partnership, the rules you grew up with may be different from your partner's. You can combine the rules and adapt them to your relationship. As it grows and stabilizes, you can adjust the guidelines accordingly. Constant communication is essential.

If you start with the agreement that feeling safe is a top priority in your relationship, it will allow you to be vulnerable and authentic with yourself and your partner. If you both are truly committed to this relationship, both of you will discover a great deal about yourselves, which will enable you to heal your past.

We haul around memories of our past relationships, like scars and souvenirs. When we get into a new relationship, we pull out our relics, and use them as a warning system to alert us whenever our partner's actions remind us of our past relationships. We hope for the best, but look for the worst.

Self discovery is the most important part of healing and understanding. Learning the difference between "reacting" and "responding" is an essential part of this process. Reaction is something that we pull out of our backpack that was used in past situations. Our reaction is instantaneous, and doesn't include thinking or planning. When we react in a relationship, it confines us to old behavior. There is no opportunity for growth, just repetitive action.

Most of us are stuck between our parent's beliefs and a new demand to be emotionally authentic to ourselves and our partner. Here we are with the backpack again. There is so much in it that needs to be cleaned out. Challenges in our relationships demand us to look at what we are carrying. This is our opportunity to heal and grow.

When we experience compassion and love for ourselves, it opens a doorway for us to feel compassion and love for our partner. All of us have a dramatic past, filled with fear, pain, frustration, sadness, and loss. We have also experienced passion, love, joy, success, and excitement.

What's in your backpack?

Chapter III - Relationships

The Wounded Parent

Parenting is one of the most complicated challenges you will ever experience. Having total responsibility for another human being is enormous and confusing. If we are still wounded from our past when a child arrives in our life, then we will raise our child from this unbalanced state.

It is our responsibility to be the best role model we can be, for our children. The foundation for parenting is strongest by our example. We must represent the balance they need. We must guide them by love, stability, and respect. Every aspect of our life is a model for our children. They force us to be honest with ourselves. We teach them with every action, word, and emotion that we express.

We have the opportunity to really look at our lives and determine what we want to change in ourselves. Our unhealed wounds are obvious when we have children who are not yet afraid to question our actions. Children speak the simple truths they see, until we tell them *not* to. Children are not born with fear; it is something we teach them.

Since we have all come from diverse backgrounds with different levels of dysfunction, it is very important to get some training and discover some tools for raising our children. There are hundreds of programs and books available to assist everyone in just about any situation.

I want to approach the subjects of technology and sports. One of the most ignored subjects is overstimulation. Adults and children are addicted to constant mental and physical stimulation.

I met a little boy one summer that had an emotional collapse during a T-Ball game. He had missed the ball three times and he just fell apart. He had trouble falling asleep and staying asleep.

When his mother brought him to visit me at my office, he seemed like a very normal energetic five-year-old. I noticed he became bored quickly and distracted easily. I asked his mother to list a typical week in his life. I noticed that all of his time was filled with continuous activities. There was no slow time or time free from outside stimulation. I asked if she would bring him by my house over the weekend for about an hour, so we could sit outside and talk.

One beautiful Saturday afternoon, Tommy came over. We took a walk, hand in hand, down the hill to the apple tree that grows alongside the creek in my back yard. We sat on an old bench, in the shade of the tree. Tommy fidgeted around for awhile and kept asking, "What are we going to do?" "Where is my mom?"

After awhile, I asked him to just listen and tell me what he heard. "Just look and tell me what you see. Just feel and tell me what you feel. Just smell, and tell me what you smell. Can you smell the water, grass, and apples? Can you hear the water flowing, the birds chirping or the leaves moving in the trees? Can you feel the wind moving through your hair, and over your skin?" I asked him to take his shoes off and feel the grass under his feet. "How does it feel?"

He picked up a stick and we dug up some dirt, smelled it, and then wiggled our toes in it. We heard a woodpecker across the creek, which created wonderment. We went closer to the creek and peeked at the bugs, looked for little fish, and then watched fallen leaves drift by us. We went back to the bench and just sat. He began to get sleepy and I could finally feel he was really relaxing.

It is so important to keep balance in our children's lives. We are extremely consumed by stimulation in our lives; we can no longer hear our inner guidance, nor feel our inner peace.

Listen to The Silence.

Who are you?

All of us define ourselves through titles and the roles we play. When this happens before we discover who we are, we do not develop our full capacity to be the creative masters we are meant to be. We play roles and hide behind masks that are controlled by the Ego. When this occurs, the Soul's development through the heart becomes immature and we do not learn how to love fully. Without self-love being fully developed, we look for love to be filled from the outside world. We use our identities to seek approval from other people. We become chameleons, constantly changing our identity to fit a situation to incur acceptance and love.

Since most people are at this stage of their evolution, it is no surprise that becoming a parent offers another mask for them to wear. There is a great distortion when it comes to parenting. Parents, who use their children as a form of identification, end up manipulating the child's life through control. When a child's natural creative power is taken away from them at an early age (because the parents are using the child as an identity booster), the child's ability to develop self-love and self-worth is destroyed. Most children will become submissive, withdrawn, or aggressive, because their development is stagnated. Children will begin to act out in many ways because they are not fully developing in a naturally balanced way.

If a child spends its younger years as an extension of their parent's identity, then upon becoming a teenager, they will fight for their own identity and power. This is why you see teenagers making dangerous choices in their lives. After spending a lifetime as an extension of one's parents, one has no foundation in place in order to guide one's choices. No foundation to stand on. It is like handing a young adult a live grenade without including the instructions. They have no frame of reference in which to make educated choices for themselves. They only know they don't want to imitate their parents.

I often see parents who have not become self-aware, who expect their children to know what's best, looking to their children for answers, or not taking on the parental role, but the role of best friend. This is another example of seeking love outside of ourselves. Being a parent shouldn't be just another mask. It is a commitment to another Soul. Parenting is one of the most challenging experiences anyone will ever have. If *you* are not self-aware, how do you expect to raise a child with self awareness?

Children fall into the same trap as their parents, seeking love and approval from the outside world. This approval comes from being judged on their behavior to determine their self worth and how they fit into the world. If the parents are wearing a mask, then early on, the children will create a mask too.

Children are very intuitive and can see through all the masks people wear. They will ask a direct question and then be confused when they hear lies. Children realize how we hide behind our own fears. What an emotional

Chapter III - Relationships

roller coaster life becomes for a child who looks to everyone else to tell them if they are lovable or not. They look towards a parent to tell them the truth and to help them learn to be authentic with their emotions. When a parent is not authentic with themselves, the lesson taught is how to disregard one's emotional self.

Sometimes when people feel their life is empty, they decide unconsciously to have children so they can experience the fullness of life and love. After experiencing a lifetime of distorted love, many people see children as an opportunity to create a human companion whom they can design exclusively to fit into their controlled world.

Masks are used by the Ego as a disguise for the personality. The Ego has no identity of its own because it was created in The Illusion. You must heal your past and take your personal journey into self discovery.

What mask are you wearing now?

Chapter III - Relationships

99

Relationships of the Future

Old partnerships revolved around our need to have a sexual partner and to populate the planet. A man needed someone to create a home, to take care of his personal needs, and to raise his children. A woman needed someone she could nurture and who would support her. Marriage was a social status. As we evolved, men and women became more independent, and our partnerships took on different priorities.

There are enough people on the planet now, so procreation isn't the main function of partnerships. As we evolve and become more balanced, there will be many changes in what we seek for our relationships. They will become a common ground for self-discovery where we can discover our highest aspirations. They will also become a place to practice the mastery of our creative process.

Think about it, you can have a partnership where you feel completely safe to be your best and to be your worst.

Relationships are the playground for the Soul. Partnerships of the future will not be committed through bondage, need, control, pride, and Ego. Partnerships will come from a foundation of love, respect, exploration, and unity.

Pure love is so rare at this time in our evolution, because we have not yet discovered self-love. Pure love is love without need. When you bring need into a partnership, love will fall away to make room for need. The moment you move into need, you begin the game of manipulation to fulfill your needs.

The possibilities for our relationships to evolve are tremendous at this time. It takes a brave person to move beyond the fear that is expressed in our reality. People who are courageous and focused will be able to move beyond their fear. When you understand that all of your power is contained in your focus, you will discover how infinite your creations can be.

Energy moves into the future to create the thoughts you have in this moment.

Bringing Balance to the Sexes

Creating balance between women and men has been a challenge from the beginning of time. Since we mainly focus from the Ego, there is always a need for superiority. The Ego is not a team player by nature.

We fight for power in our relationships. Nowhere on this planet is there complete balance between the sexes. Some countries are worse than others. The belief of many religions that God is male implies superiority of that gender.

Men and women are designed to complement each other, using their power to support the development of one another. Since there is really no separation between us, then the more I support you in your evolution, the more "I" evolve. Together, we assist the evolution of humanity.

Think for a moment about The Illusion of separation. It is important for us to see beyond The Illusion, in order for our species to evolve. As long as we believe in separation, this world will be in chaos. As long as there are "us" and "them," there will be wars. Humanity has been unconscious for such a long time that the thought of Oneness is incomprehensible. That is why it is so important for us to understand the concept of separation in The Illusion.

Whether there are billions of people, or only ten, it must be understood. For our species to evolve, we must move from our Ego state of survival to conscious Oneness. We must pull our attention inward, away from The Illusion. We must reconnect to our Souls to find our wisdom. If we don't reconnect with our Souls, humanity as we know it will not survive.

If you think you have limitations, then you will.

Chapter III - Relationships

Sex in the Future

As our relationships begin to take on a different focus, so will our approach to sex. At the present stage of our evolution, most of our sexual actions come through the focus of the Ego. Our instinctive expression of sex is very goal oriented. We are basically focused on arriving at the end of the action, which is the climax.

All of the actions leading up to the climax are solely focused on getting to the climax. When sex becomes a race, you severely limit your experience. Since the focus is on a specific goal (what is happening between our legs), we do not take the time to connect fully and expand our awareness.

What if I told you that the outcome of sex is not the climax? What if you knew that the journey to the climax is where an expansion of consciousness happens? In an expanded state, every cell in your body can experience the climax.

In this expanded state, the space between you and your partner virtually disappears. A deeper form of ecstasy is experienced.

When you take time to awaken all of your senses, the climax will expand throughout your entire body. We have six senses that can be heightened during a physical encounter. If you take the time to fully awaken each one of the six, to the peak of its stimulation, you will experience bliss.

Many people are seeking this expansion in their sexual experience. Women, in particular, want more intimacy in their partnerships--they want a complete experience.

There is a large difference between having sex and making love. Having sex is goal orientated, and making love takes patience and total awareness in the moment. You can only make love if you stay in the moment. In that experience, there is nowhere to go, nowhere to be, just floating in the very action and reactions that are going on between you and your partner.

Chapter III - Relationships   107

In our present stage of evolution this kind of experience is rare, because we feel so vulnerable when we open ourselves up to this degree. We are still so afraid of our partners and of ourselves.

To evolve, we must move through our fears.

Chapter III - Relationships

The Challenges We Face

Our evolution depends on balance. Humanity is experiencing a tremendous surge toward balance. All of us have equal amounts of feminine and masculine energy flowing naturally in our body. Society has assigned each sex a specific role that defines us as a gender. We perpetually struggle to fit this role through our Ego's drive to mold us, so we fit into society. Where the Ego succeeds in molding us for society, it also severely corrupts our true nature.

As the feminine energy seeks balance and gains momentum in the male body, a more sensitive male is created. In contrast, as the masculine energy seeks balance in the female body, a more assertive female is surfacing. This can be confusing to the personality of the male and the female.

The Ego has limited knowledge from The Illusion to identify confusion and categorize it. We must identify our actions and feelings to reinforce the personality. Men are going through such a huge transformation as this feminine energy seeks balance. They are confused as to what the rules are that define them as men. Men are seeking women who are independent and less of a responsibility. Women demand that men offer more in their relationships, requiring them to be more sensitive and open to a partnership that is balanced. This has created challenges for both partners.

What people want in relationships is more equality and better communication. As women become more independent and self-sufficient in society, they are less willing to settle for a relationship that isn't satisfying. Men are seeking women who are not so dependent and helpless. As we move further away from the typical structured relationship, the more we will focus on personal development through partnerships.

All Life is Precious.

Chapter IV

Illness, Death and Coming Full Circle

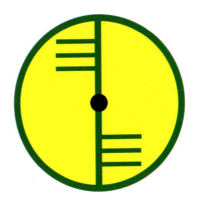

The Pain of Death

I have held death in my arms.

I have seen a last breath.

I have felt my heart explode from grief.

I have felt I could not take
my next breath.

Yes, death and I know each other well.

My mind says, "It's time to celebrate,"
my love has just been born into another
realm, beginning a new journey.

I cannot see this other realm,
but I know it exists.

There is no death of the Soul, this I know.

What I don't know is how to pull the
shards of glass from my heart, to ease
the pain and stop the bleeding.

The Ultimate Imbalance

The ultimate imbalance manifests in the physical body, as disease. Over the years I have met people who were able to *conquer* their disease, and many who were conquered *by* their disease. There are many factors involved in the manifestation of disease, as well as many factors involved in the creation of a cure.

Each person is unique; we can only speculate and generalize about the cause of disease and how to bring about a cure. However, I do know that when a person is faced with a disease in their body, whatever that individual was doing up to that moment in time, is what has caused the disease to manifest in their life. If you create a disease, then you can create good health as well.

Every human being has the potential to grow a disease in his or her body. At this stage of our evolution, with our various degrees of disconnection, disease will continue to manifest. We are fragmented in The Illusion, due to our belief of separation. This belief of separation keeps us in a weakened state. Disease is only possible in The Illusion.

Your body believes everything your mind tells it. If you become your disease, it will become you. You must never think that you are the disease. Just like the salad you ate yesterday and flushed away this morning, your disease is not you, it just moves through you. Disease has a low and dense vibration. In contrast, a healthy body vibrates at a high frequency. Make your body uninhabitable for the disease, by raising your vibration too high for the disease to live within you.

Everything you think, say, and do, must reflect your highest vibrations. All of your senses must vibrate with love, with every aspect of love there is--everything that brings you true joy, must fill every second of your life. Make the connection to your Soul strong and clear, so you will be guided through all of your choices in every day. Working with your wisdom, live life to its fullest, whether you have one day or one hundred years.

Death only takes a second. You are living life up until the second of your death. How you live your life, until the second of your death, is what gives your life meaning. Your death does not define your life. How you die, and when you die is what you leave behind as memories for others.

The question is not *if* you want to live, but *how* you want to live. Your Soul needs a reason to stay and a body to live in. Your Soul needs a way to feel its connection to the Oneness. Fragmentation, our mistaken belief that we are somehow separate from Source, is what makes that connection weak.

Every person who has lived through an experience with a serious disease has one thing in common. They have each been given the opportunity to see their life in a larger context. Our bodies were never meant to be permanent. We must live today like our death is tomorrow.

People that have experienced a serious disease understand this, and that understanding has strengthened their ability to live with Soul.

Thought is Source in motion.

Death is a New Beginning

Death is a transformation. Death is simply a process of change. We tend to focus so much on our experience on earth, that we constrict this inner knowing. We have lost our connection with the wisdom of our Soul. If we can expand our belief about death in this way, we can reconnect to our inner wisdom, which amplifies our awareness.

To illustrate my point, imagine that you are driving a car down a country road. In this example, the car will represent your physical body. Suddenly your car engine stops. You leave the car and begin to walk down the road noticing an oasis by the side of the road.

You walk over to the oasis, to refresh and heal yourself. There, you drink the fresh water, and cleanse yourself in the spring. You are able to swim in the cool water, which refreshes your Soul. There is an abundance of food for you to eat, and you feel rejuvenated. There is a shaded place for you to rest. This gives your Soul an opportunity to carefully choose your next experience.

When you are fully recovered, you continue down the road. You come to a tunnel, which represents your next experience. As you pass through the tunnel, you discover another car is waiting for you. You get into this new car, and continue on with your journey. It is a different vehicle, a different time, a different reality, and a different purpose. Now, what if you did this for eternity? This is a very simplistic way of looking at our death, yet it has a feeling of continuous movement.

Your journey does not end just because your car breaks down. In fact, getting a different vehicle gives you the opportunity to redefine the details of your new journey. Your experience is always evolution through creation. We do not die when our body dies.

The dream is: you are here.

Chapter IV - Illness, Death and Coming Full Circle   123

You Came in Naked and You Will Leave Naked

Death is one of the most fantastic experiences we are able to have, while we are in a physical body. If you are lucky enough to live a long life, and have an idea when it is your time to leave, then you can prepare for your journey. You can choose to leave in peace.

If you are given the opportunity to prepare for this journey, then make the most of this gift. Let go of all the possessions you have accumulated in this life. You came in naked, and you will leave naked. I like to compare the experience of death to the experience of moving.

Most of us have moved from one house to another at least once in our lives. Each time we move, we sort through our possessions, and decide what we want and don't want any more. We give special things away to our friends as gifts. We donate other items to charity. Some things we just throw away. Whether you are leaving your body or moving, letting go lightens your load, and helps you prepare for a new experience.

Discarding your body, and moving on, should be a celebration. It should not be something to dread and fear. If you have a disease that is causing pain, there are a variety of medications available to help you manage your pain so you are able to stay focused on your experience. Visualize the process of disconnecting from your body, and witness the transformation of death. Unless you have an untimely death, this preparation process can be a profound experience.

We are eternal consciousness moving from one experience to the next. We are focused on this experience while we are here, but once our body is not available, we will focus on our next experience. We use our bodies for this dimensional plane of existence. Try and view your visit here as if it were a vacation from where you were.

Chapter IV - Illness, Death and Coming Full Circle 125

In this sense, if you are in the process of dying, then it is time to get out the party hats. It is time to have a bon voyage party to celebrate your journey. Invite all your family and friends, have lots of food and music, and start giving away all your things. Sell your house, move into a perfect dream apartment. Get something furnished, or go out and buy whatever you want. What a pleasure it would be to shop totally for yourself, with no one to impress.

You can have anything you ever wanted. Make your will. Get everything in order, and enjoy the rest of your life. Wear purple, wear red or go naked, whatever you want. If you have a limited income, you can still have fun. Have a raffle, or auction off your things. Have your friends over to play cards.

You will experience such freedom when you begin to let go of your possessions. We spend our lifetime accumulating things. Many people believe that all of these possessions define who they are in this world. We are so much more than our "stuff."

126   Living with Soul ⊕ Linda Jane Becker

Always remember that when you leave "here," all of your needs will be taken care of when you arrive "there." It is our intense attachment to our possessions that actually plays a very big part in how we experience the process of dying. Holding on can be very painful.

You may think that you would not be able to do this, that it would be too hard to let go of everything while you are still alive. This exact thinking is what causes so much pain when a person is in the process of dying. Your belief that you cannot do something is the greatest destroyer of who you really are. Who you are is an "unlimited creator." You can think of hundreds of reasons why this wouldn't work for you, or you can use that same energy to modify your life situation, and make it work. Remember you never have to go through it alone. You can always ask for help.

If you are afraid to do something, it is important for you to ask yourself, "Why am I afraid?" You will discover that your fear really has nothing to do with you, unless you are self-judging. It has more to do with how you think other people will judge you.

Ask yourself, "Can I walk completely away from my life right now?" If you said no, then realize you still have attachments in this life. You receive freedom by letting go.

Sometimes we are concerned about the people we are leaving behind, worried how our death will affect them. Help them understand that you are not really leaving them, and that your relationship with them will only be in a different context.

Not being attached to this life doesn't make you uninvolved. It frees you so you are no longer controlled by the fear of life or death.

Just keep saying *yes* to life! Once you are gone, what does any of this matter anyway? Will any of this matter one hundred years from now?

Make a list of all the things you would like to do before you die, and then start doing those things today. For example, if you have always wanted to kiss the baker at the local grocery store, then go get your kiss. Nothing works quite so well as asking someone to honor a dying wish. It works almost every time. If it doesn't work, then know that at least you tried, cross it off your list, and go on to the next thing. Keep moving forward, keep living life.

Lighten up. You don't have to be so serious; life is meant to be fun. Your whole life is comprised of the choices you make, and how you process those choices. If you want to be a miserable old person, wanting to make your dying process difficult for yourself and everyone else, go ahead. Remember, in one hundred years, who will care? It won't matter to you once you're out of here.

A friend of mine often complains about the fullness of her plate. She insists she will enjoy life when this or that is done. And over the years, I have watched her plate remain full. As soon as she removes one thing, something else jumps in to take its place. I call this, waiting for the creek to dry up so I can cross.

Are you stuck waiting to start your life? Do you tell yourself that you will start living when something is completed, or that you can start breathing when it is done? A full plate only means you have an active life.

You have a choice of what goes on your plate. You also are allowed to put "personal" things on your plate. Take a walk in the park, soak in a hot tub, and savor breakfast in bed. You can even make the choice to enjoy a whole day without the outside world intruding.

It is so important to enjoy your life every day. Don't postpone it until tomorrow, because tomorrow doesn't exist. There is only today. You will discover, if you look deep enough inside your excuses, that all excuses boil down to one simple fact; you are afraid to live fully.

I have worked with many people over the years, and I can say that the majority of them only needed permission to live their lives. I've listened for hours to people go on about their limitations, of how they've painted themselves into a corner. Most of the problems people have are due to their personal stagnation. They won't make a new choice. The decision to not make a new choice is still a choice. You can choose not to choose.

People love to blame other people or situations for their unhappiness. Always remember that this whole illusion is only your perception of it.

My father used to tell me, "One man's trash is another man's treasure." Over the years, I have come to understand this in so many ways. Someone may think you are lucky to have such a wonderful life, while at the same time, you might think your life is terrible. Absolutely everything is experienced through our perception.

Years ago, on the days I would feel sorry for myself, I would sit down and write a list of all the wonderful things in my life. This would always remind me of my current good fortune. What did I have to be depressed about? Most of my depression came from my past and involved people and situations that I blamed for my misery. If I had chosen not to drag the past into my present moment, I wouldn't have had any fuel for my misery. This was an exquisite discovery. Stay in the present, and all is well.

Imagine that in this moment, you have a toothache. While you are experiencing pain in this moment, it will motivate you into making a choice to remove yourself from the pain. You could take some pain medication until you can get to the dentist. Another choice would be to drag your past into the present by fanning the fires of fault. You could blame yourself for not taking good care of your teeth. You could blame your parents for not giving you better teeth, or teaching you better hygiene. The list could go on and on. We use "the blame game" when we do not want to take responsibility for what is going on in our life. It seems easier to point fingers at someone or something else, instead of taking responsibility for our own lives.

When I work with people who have experienced a violent crime, one of the hardest things to help them understand is that they were victimized yesterday, or last year, or twenty years ago, but they are not a victim right now. The path to healing is deciding not to be a victim today.

Healing your past begins with your decision to not drag the past into the present. If your body has been injured, then your focus needs to be on healing that injured part of you. If your mind has been injured, then you need to let go of the memories. If we would start each day like it is a new beginning, we would not carry the past into the present. Many times, I ask my students, who are stuck in their past, "What if you woke up tomorrow morning and had total amnesia?" The first thing they feel is great relief. Then they feel lost and afraid, because they don't have a history to define who they are.

The life they are living today is defined by the life they lived yesterday--living in the past and not moving into the future.

Why do we bring the past into the present moment? We do it because we created the person we are, from the history we have experienced. This, we've decided, is our identity. We become our history, by developing a personality that reflects our past, not our present.

Imagine how free we would feel if we started each day with amnesia. We could allow ourselves to wake up daily to a fresh start, a new perspective, a new life. Our past sets up patterns that we haul into the future. We experience the same old behavior, the same old thoughts, and the same old day.

Is it any wonder that so many people like to buy material things to fill their lives? These people continually need something new so that they can feel alive. Something new feels good only for a short time.

This type of excitement is fleeting. The fact is we can create a whole new view of our lives just by perceiving it differently. It isn't "stuff" that makes us feel good. We crave the stimulation we feel as the stuff attracts our focus and fills our emptiness. It's a distraction from our previous focus. After awhile, the emptiness only swallows up our stuff, and we feel empty again, so we start looking for something to fill the void--again.

What we desire is to feel the fullness of our true self, the self that is not experiencing separation. We only suffer because we believe in The Illusion of separation. If you see beyond The Illusion, and connect to the wholeness of who you are, there is no suffering. If you can see beyond The Illusion, you will see that your body is not who you are. Your body is only a vehicle that you use for your travels, and you use it for such a short duration. See beyond The Illusion, and choose each day to be new and exciting.

Chapter IV - Illness, Death and Coming Full Circle 135

We aren't here to save the world, or to go down in the history books. Most of the history books aren't accurate anyway; they end up being the perception of the writer. The person telling the story is having an experience which they judge and define with their own beliefs and perceptions. The Illusion is like a mirage. Do you see how intangible life really is?

When you speak of the past, ask yourself, "Where is it?" The past is only an electrical impulse in your brain. If you stop acknowledging an old thought long enough, it disappears. If you stop energizing the thought by letting go of your focus on it, the old thought will dissolve. How real is it now?

Anything in your past is no longer valid if you don't bring it into the present moment and re-energize it with your thoughts. Imagine a leaf floating down a stream. When the energy of the current stops, the leaf will sink and dissolve. Your thoughts are the same way. Let them go, let the current take them away so they can dissolve.

The people that you choose to spend your time with will affect you in many ways. It is your choice who you allow into your life. Be selective in the company you keep, even if it is your family. Are you creating a life full of success, joy, fun, adventure and love? It is necessary to surround yourself with people who desire the same things.

You can detach from your family if they are not supporting your life in a positive way. You can choose not to have them be a part of your life. You can divorce your original family and adopt another one that supports your life choices. Society may not agree with this, but you always have a choice of who you invite into your life every day.

We must all learn that we are never stuck in any situation. We are only stuck in fear. Our biggest fear is the fear of change. This is actually ironic, as in this illusion there is nothing *but* change. Energy changes form, every second of every day. It amazes me how people will stay in an unpleasant situation, only because they are afraid to change it.

If you are miserable today with a situation, then try again tomorrow. If you are still miserable tomorrow, make a choice to change the situation. Never forget that you have the power of infinite choice.

We are swimming in a sea of energy.

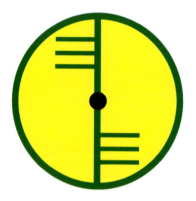

The Disk of Potentiality

The symbol you have seen throughout this book is called "The Disk of Potentiality." During a deep meditation in The Silence, I was gifted the disk to share with humanity. It will create a doorway into The Silence for you, which will assist and accelerate your personal evolution.

Before you do your meditations, look at the disk for a minute or so, then close your eyes and see the disk in your mind's eye. When you are ready, go through the black hole in the center, this will lead you into The Silence.

At first you may only be able to stay for a few seconds, but the more you practice, the longer you can stay, until your whole meditation is in The Silence.

Use the disk every time you want to connect deeply with your Soul. It is very powerful and can assist you in many ways. The disk represents a keyhole and "you" are the key.

142　　　Living with Soul ⊕ Linda Jane Becker

Chapter V

Meditations

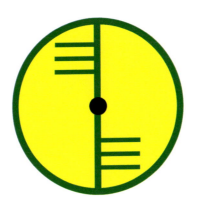

144 Living with Soul ⊕ Linda Jane Becker

The Mask

Always a mask
Held in the slim hand whitely.
Always, she had a mask before her face-
Truly the wrist
Holding it lightly
Fitted the task:
Sometimes however
Was there a shiver?
Fingertip quiver,
Ever so slightly-
Holding the mask
For years and years I wondered
But dared not ask
And then-
I blundered,
Looked behind the mask,
To find
Nothing-
She had no face.
She had become

Merely a hand
Holding a mask with grace.

Author Unknown

Let's Meditate

Meditation helps us connect to our Soul. If you are quiet enough and listen, you can discover the answers to all of your questions.

In this book, I have given you a variety of meditations from which to choose. It is useful to first read through the meditations, to familiarize yourself with the selections. All of the meditations are designed to be modified to your personal needs. Change whatever you feel fits your situation. Be creative in your design. The more often you do each meditation, the more personal it will become. After awhile it will take less time for you to get relaxed and clear enough, so that you can slip into your special space. Be open to experiences that may not be logical to your rational mind.

When you are ready to do a meditation, find a quiet place to relax. It is best to sit in a comfortable chair. If you lie down, you have a greater chance of falling asleep before you complete your meditation. "The Raft" meditation is used for sleeping. This meditation should be started after you are lying comfortably in bed.

Scanning and relaxing your body is an essential part of meditation. Slowing down your thinking will be your greatest challenge.

I like to use the sound of water to help put me in a relaxed state. Much of my time is spent in various states of meditation. I have water fountains inside and outside my home. There is a creek in my back yard where I can sit under an apple tree to be with nature. Having a quiet place where you can go is as important as the air you breathe. You must spend part of your life away from the stimulation of civilization. You must connect with your Soul. If you live in the city, there are parks you can visit.

If you live in an apartment complex, you can create a sanctuary within your living space. The best choice would be to design an extra room for your meditations. If you don't have the luxury of an extra room, turn your bedroom into a sanctuary. You'll be surprised how well you can sleep.

Pillows and blankets will help you feel comfortable, and set the mood. Fill the room with live plants. Place a small table within view, and set a candle in the middle. Put items that bring you joy around the candle. Light the candle before each meditation, to set your focus. Make it fun, choosing things for your table. This room is alive with your intent. The more you use your space the more magical it will become.

Playing a CD that is relaxing can be very helpful in muffling sounds from the outside. Your best choice of music is music without lyrics. Do not choose music that stimulates past memories. Keeping your mind as clear as possible is extremely important.

Connecting with your Soul takes dedication and patience. It is important to devote time every morning and every evening for this practice. Even if you only have ten minutes a day, that's a good start. Meditation creates a fantastic expansion in your reality. It empowers you to create and brings great peace.

Breathing Deep
  Finding Your Center

Find a comfortable place to relax your body to do this meditation. Take a couple of deep breaths, and bring your focus into the moment. Scan your body from top to bottom, looking for any tension you might be feeling. When you find a place that feels tense, focus directly on it, and release the tightness. Do this throughout your body, until you are completely relaxed.

Deep breathing is the best exercise for getting your body to slow down and relax. At first, just sit comfortably, and observe your breathing. Witness your inhale and exhale. You will feel the tension and stress leaving your body. Just breathe. When you feel relaxed, start breathing deeper, exhale normally.

Repeat the deep breaths three times, and then go back to your normal breathing for several breaths. Continue doing this pattern until you are too relaxed to breathe deeply. When you open your eyes, you will be extremely relaxed and centered in peace.

Chapter V - Meditations   151

Erasing the Lines of The Illusion
Connecting with Oneness

To fully understand consciousness and to comprehend the Oneness that we are; you first must be able to experience beyond The Illusion. You must be able to rest in your Soul.

One of the greatest gifts my Soul has given me is this exercise. It helps me go beyond The Illusion. It is important for you to experience the Source that is within you. G.O.D., Go Only Deep, is always accessible within you. Reconnecting with Source can fertilize your Soul for greater expansion. Expanding your awareness is the only way you can open up to infinity, which is what we are.

Find a comfortable place to relax your body to do this meditation. It must be void of distracting sounds. Take a couple of deep breaths, and bring your focus into this moment.

I want you to pay attention to your breathing. Do not change your breathing, because this is not a breathing exercise. Just breathe. Feel your breath enter and exit your body. Don't think, just feel.

I want you to imagine you have an eraser in your hand. This special eraser is for erasing The Illusion. Remember that I define Illusion as the experience of separation from Source.

Start erasing all the lines that represent The Illusion to you. Start by erasing your body. Then erase whatever you are sitting on, erase everything you remember in the room. Begin erasing the whole building, city, state, country, continent, and planet. Erase everything in space until all lines of separation are gone. You will begin to feel how you have expanded. You will become the Oneness with Source. There will be no separation, only infinity. This is who you are without the lines.

You can stay in this bliss for as long as you like. It is a wonderful place to fall asleep. You will wake up and feel very peaceful. Your world will look differently, and feel differently. If you do not want to go to sleep, and you are basically doing this to balance yourself, then the road back to The Illusion is simply to replace the lines.

Once you have mastered this meditation, you can use it several times a day to center yourself. Getting a perspective on The Illusion by stepping out of it is the best way to stay conscious.

Letting Go
  Releasing Thoughts and Memories

Find a comfortable place to relax your body to do this meditation. Take a couple of deep breaths, and bring your focus into this moment. Scan your body from top to bottom, looking for any tension you are feeling. When you find a place that feels tense, focus directly on it, and release the tightness. Do this throughout your body until you are completely relaxed.

This meditation is for letting go of memories and emotions that are interfering with your evolution. In this vision, you should be sitting by the side of a creek, completely surrounded by dry, fallen autumn leaves. The sounds of their crispness fill your ears every time you move. The creek is moving at a steady pace, as it disappears into the distance.

As you sit, notice the thoughts which pass through your mind. Pick up a leaf, and place each thought on a leaf. Lean over, and place the leaf in the flowing water. Watch the leaf drift away, and feel the release your body

Chapter V - Meditations   155

is experiencing. Let go of each thought as you watch the leaf move with the current, as it leaves your sight. Repeat this with all of the memories, emotions, and thoughts which you brought into this meditation.

This is the best meditation for cleaning and clearing your mind. I do this every night, so that I don't drag unresolved issues into my dreams or into the next day. My dreams are extremely important to me, because that is where I receive the majority of my knowledge. I also want my next day to be clear and fresh. If an issue needs more consideration, I know it will present itself again.

Rainbow River Chakra Clearing
  Cleaning Out Your Energetic System

Find a comfortable place to relax your body to do this meditation. Take a couple of deep breaths, and bring your focus into this moment. Scan your body from top to bottom looking for any tension you are feeling. When you find a place that feels tense, focus directly on it, and release the tightness. Do this throughout your body until you are completely relaxed.

I want you to see in your mind, a winding dirt path leading into the forest. You are standing on this path in your bare feet. The path is warm from the sunshine. You can feel the soft, fine dirt pressing against the bottom of your feet. You feel this warmth moving up your body, warming and relaxing every muscle, as it travels from the bottom of your feet to the top of your head.

You begin to stroll down this path. You notice the sounds, the colors, and the warmth of the wind as it caresses your skin. You feel very safe and at peace. As you enter the forest,

Chapter V - Meditations   157

you can see the sunlight filtering through the branches, lighting your way. The air becomes cooler with the shade. A deep peacefulness fills your body.

You feel as if you are a part of the forest. You feel totally safe. The path leads to a clearing in the trees. As you walk through this clearing you see a stream. This stream is filled with fresh water. The sun is shining on the water, giving it an illuminating glow. The stream flows as far as you can see, in both directions. You walk out into the center of the water, and face downstream.

The water whirls around your ankles, feeling gentle and refreshing. You feel the light of the sun filling your head. As the light travels down through your body cleaning out your chakras, you can see a black liquid pouring out of the tips of your toes. When all of your chakras are cleared, sunlight will come out of your toes.

Now with your chakras completely cleared out, turn around and face upstream. As you look upstream you see a rainbow melting into the stream. You see the colors flowing towards you, one at a time.

You notice a beautiful illuminated white light, with flakes of gold shimmering in it. The white light approaches your toes, and moves up your body until it reaches the top of your head. Next, you see the color indigo flowing into your toes, moving up to the chakra between your eyes. Blue travels up your body to your throat. Green moves up to your heart chakra. Yellow fills your solar plexus. Orange fills your pelvis area. Red empowers your root chakra, at the end of your tailbone. The rainbow has completely filled your body.

You are now feeling totally balanced and in harmony. You cross to the other side of the stream. You see a hammock tied between two trees. You dry your feet off in the grass and climb into the hammock. You lay comfortably as it gently sways in the wind. You are in total peace.

The Raft Meditation
To Induce Sleep

Find a comfortable place to relax your body to do this meditation. Take a couple of deep breaths, and bring your focus into this moment. Scan your body from top to bottom, looking for any tension you are feeling. When you find a place that feels tense, focus directly on it, and release the tightness. Do this throughout your body, until you are completely relaxed.

I want you to see in your mind, a beautiful pond in front of you. This pond is small and filled with crystal clear water. You can see sparkling white sand on the bottom. It is only about two feet deep, and completely still. It is late afternoon, on a summer day. The temperature of the air is perfect.

Tall trees surround the pond, giving you a feeling of total peace and safety. You can hear the wind as it gently moves through the trees. You are sitting on a bench at the water's edge. Remove your shoes, and put your toes in the water.

Chapter V - Meditations

The water feels warm, like a bath. Feeling totally relaxed and at peace, you can see a raft floating in front of you. It moves closer to you nudging your feet, inviting you to climb on. You gently climb on, lying on your back.

The raft is soft and comforting. You can see the blue sky through the tops of the trees. The raft begins to drift away from the shore. You feel totally safe and completely relaxed. You are drifting around the pond. You are at peace. It is time for you to rest.

Last Words From The Author

I have given you many tools that will assist you in changing your life. Own your power and choose to create a wonderful life for yourself. Everyone you know will be curious to learn how you are doing it. As our lives change through our creative power, we will see a change in the world. We are in the midst of *The Great Spiritual Revolution.*

I hope you have found some of the answers you were looking for. My intent was to shine a light upon *my* truth to guide you to *your* truth. It is extremely important for you to own your creative power. Use it to guide you towards your passion. Use it to create a reality that brings you joy, love and peace. Let's change the world together by *Living with Soul.* I hope I have served you well.

Engulfed by the Light
Linda Jane Becker

164   Living with Soul ⊕ Linda Jane Becker

About The Author

For over twenty years I studied and trained in healing techniques from around the world. I traveled to India, Nepal, and Hawaii to attain my highest level of training. I perfected my own healing program and for ten years, I had three offices in the Portland, Oregon area. My centers were open to everyone on a donation basis. My work included thousands of healing sessions with hundreds of patients. I taught alternative healing classes at Portland Community College and private meditations classes to public figures.

For the past five years, I have devoted my life to writing, which provides the opportunity to share my knowledge on a grander scale. I live in the Pacific Northwest with my husband and several mischievous cats.

Credentials

1987.................. Hypnosis and Meditation
1987.................. School of Metaphysics
1988.................. Past Life Regression Training
1989.................. Shamanic Soul Retrieval
1993.................. REIKI Usui Shiki Ryotto 1&2
1994.................. Healing Touch 1&2
1994.................. University of Science and Philosophy
1994.................. SHEN Therapy
1996.................. Flower of Life Training
1997.................. Marriage of Spirit Training
1998.................. Bio-Magnetic Touch Healing
1999.................. Tibetan Shamanic Training
2000.................. Toltec Shamanic Training
2000.................. Huna Healing Training
2000.................. REIKI Mastership Training
2001.................. Universal Life Church Ministry
2001.................. Yuen Energetics 1, 2&3
2002.................. Advanced Nepali Shamanic Healing
2002.................. Remote Viewing Training
2003.................. Reconnection Healing 1, 2&3

Contact Information

Linda Jane Becker
    LivingWithSoulFoundation.com
    Disk of Potentiality.com
    LindaJaneBecker.com
    LindaJaneBecker@gmail.com

Mailing Address:
    Linda Jane Becker
    P.O.Box 842
    St. Helens, OR 97051

Tom Leavey
Tom Leavey .... Harmony Records
www.Toml.org

Healing CD's:
Illumination 2008
Survivors 2009

Available at:
Amazon.com
CD Baby.com

Authors Photograph
Heather L. Becker

Cover Photography:
Front .... Milton Creek, in my back yard.
Back .... my bench, under the apple tree.
Linda J. Becker
Summer 2008

Cover design:
Levon T. Becker and Heather L. Becker

The Disk of Potentiality design:
Linda Jane Becker